# THE DRUM THAT BEATS WITHIN US
*Poetry*

"Passionately felt emotional connections, particularly to Western landscapes and Native American culture... compellingly linking the great cycles of stars with little, common lives... to create a powerful sense of loss... a muscular poignancy." – *Kirkus*

"The poetry is sometimes raw, painful, exquisite but there is always the sense that it was written from the heart." – *LibraryThing*

"A collection of poetry that explores the elements of nature, what nature can provide, what nature can take away, and how humans are connected to it all." – *Book Review Bin*

"An exploration of self and nature... that asks us to look at our environment through the eyes of animals... and the poetry that has been with us since the dawn of time... comforting, challenging, and thought provoking." – *Bound2Books*

"His poetry courses, rhythmic and true through his works. His words serve as an important alarm for readers to wake from their contented slumber of self-absorbed thought and notice the changes around them. Eye-opening and a joy to read, the master of the existential thriller can add another winning title to his accolades." – *BookTrib*

"The language is beautiful, heartbreaking, romantic, sad, savvy, and nostalgic all at once. From longer poems to very short, thought-provoking poems, the lines of each take the reader to a world the poet has experienced or given much thought to. Truly beautiful." – *Goodreads*

"This is such a beautiful book of poetry ... the imagery is vibrant, devastating, and haunting... A thoroughly modern 21st century collection that revisits and revises classic themes. Highly recommended." – *NetGalley*

"The poems are beautiful and range from the long lyrical expressions of love and nature to the brief expressions of a moments insight into a sudden feeling, expressed with a few words that capture the moment and the feeling perfectly. " – *Metapsychology Reviews*

"*The Drum That Beats Within Us* presents us with a world gone awry, a world in which the warrior poet has fought, and a world in which only love survives." – *Vine Reviews*

# ALSO BY MIKE BOND

**POETRY**

The Drum That Beats Within Us

**NOVELS**

America

Freedom

Revolution

The Last Savanna

Assassins

Saving Paradise

Killing Maine

Goodbye Paris

Snow

House of Jaguar

Holy War

Tibetan Cross

*In memoriam*
*Isobelle Ray Bond*
*Was there ever a poem you didn't know?*

*Joy is the infallible sign of the presence of God.*

– Teilhard de Chardin

# JOY

*Poems of love, life, and fate*

# MIKE BOND

BIG CITY PRESS

Cover design by Alan Dingman

Author photo by © PF Bentley / PFPIX.com

MikeBondBooks.com

Published in the United States by Big City Press, New York.

ISBN PAPERBACK: 978-1-949751-30-7

ISBN EBOOK: 978-1-949751-31-4

PUBLISHER'S CATALOGING-IN-PUBLICATION DATA

Names: Bond, Mike, author.

Title: Joy : poems of love, life, and fate / Mike Bond.

Description: New York, NY: Big City Press, 2022.

Identifiers: ISBN: 978-1-949751-30-7 (paperback) | 978-1-949751-31-4 (ebook)

Subjects: LCSH Poetry, American. | BISAC POETRY / Subjects & Themes / General | POETRY / Subjects & Themes / Death, Grief, Loss | POETRY / Subjects & Themes / Family | POETRY / Subjects & Themes / Inspirational & Religious | POETRY / Subjects & Themes / Love & Erotica | POETRY / Subjects & Themes / Nature

Classification: LCC PS3602.O6565 J69 2022 | DDC 811--dc23

# CONTENTS

# PREFACE

One night years ago I had a dream of being in a large place like a supermarket, a low ceiling and aisles with shelves on both sides. I asked someone, a young guy who looked like me, "What are we here for?"

"To find out what it is," he said.

"What *what* is?"

"Life."

That, I have since realized, is perhaps our deepest goal. In the midst of this great mystery of being that we do not understand, what is most important is *To find out what it is.*

From our understanding of life, partial as it must be, comes all our other goals, to live and love deeply and well, to learn, and to sustain life, family, and all living things.

To understand life, we share our experiences, what we've learned in living. To do this we must communicate with others.

Poetry is a perfect way to share our deepest, truest experiences. So we all can learn from each others' lives.

In poetry we learn not only to communicate with others, but also with ourselves.

Which is why everyone should write poetry. It allows our deepest feelings, our unrecognized desires and wildest thoughts, to escape from the prison of our minds and the rules we impose on ourselves. To share them not only with others but with ourselves.

In that way poetry circles us back to our goal, to find out what life is.

It is an endless process, destined to be incomplete. In an infinite universe of time and space, its origin perhaps not the beginning – was there ever a beginning? – what are *we*? In our own nearly infinite cells, our vast and cloistered past and unknown future, what does it mean to be alive?

These are not frivolous questions. For they govern the very infinity of our daily thoughts and actions. They govern who we are.

Our ancestors were poets from the moment they could speak, perhaps even before, communicating non-verbally as other animals do. More recently, they made pictures on cave walls and cut statues of stone, ivory, and wood. They told stories around their fires, raised their children with tales of their ancestors, as we do today. Many ages later they wrote stories on clay tablets, then papyrus, then paper, often in rhyme.

Rhyme is a memory enhancer. It's easier to remember a line when it rhymes with an earlier one, there's a cadence, a rhythm, that keeps the story going. And before the written word, memory was the only way to preserve our histories, or stories, our past. Some of our greatest literature was first oral, then centuries later written down.

There is a marvelous infinite world out there beyond our awareness. Occasionally we get a glimpse, a sense of something far greater, more universal than ourselves, then it's gone. But poetry can break down that wall, make the glimpse longer, help us *see*.

That's why we're here, and why we write and read poetry.

To find out what life is.

# JOY

How lovely
to hold your hand,
to see your face
across a table,
a glass of wine,
a room,
to share children,
a home,
a life.
It takes so little
to bring joy
into the world.

## BURGUNDY

Sun gleams the golden stones,
green grass ripples,
vineyard and forest,
earth black
in your hand,
or red with shattered stones,
or gray-green river rock,
sun-warmed,
but cold
in winter.

Far as human
eye can see,
across this endless tiny
fragment of our universe
among so many universes,
we find no one
but ourselves.

Where are *they*?
What do they know?
Have they cleaved
the golden mystery?
Have they claimed
the unknown?

Bones, white bones among the soil
of sun-warmed Burgundy,
pitted, rotted, gone,
a thousand thousand years
of destiny and death

and love
and care
in every moment.
What do they *know*
we don't?

What did they learn
in death
we cannot learn
before?

There is love,
and care,
the warmth of another's
hand,
a look in the eye,
constant as forever,
*I love you*
*I care for you*
*no matter how many*
*universes*
*of doubt and fire,*
*I will never*
*leave you.*
*I will never*
*do you harm.*

So good to say,
we stake our universes
on it, we promise
the simple vow
of a human heart
will outlast time.

## THE DIVINE

We seek God elsewhere,
in churches and stock markets,
shopping malls, car dealers,
wars and wisdom,
while the divine is always
with us
in the face
of a loved one,
the laugh
of a child,
the joy of a dog
running wild
in the woods,
a bird singing
from a treetop,
a far view
over mountains
to the sea,
a glass of wine
or field of flowers.

The ancients were right:
God is always with us,
we just have
to notice.

## PATHWAYS OF THE HEART

We sit round the fire
in the misty tall-fir mountains,
and dream of antelope
and love,
and of living
a long time
in these valleys cloven
by ardent rivers,
grass-fragrant
rock-mossy
elegant meadows,
black forests and
peaks of rocky ice,
these pathways of the heart,
these bones of marrow
and skins so soft and warm,
in this clan
of love and family
wishing to live
forever.

## DANGER

The tiger paces
his cage,
hoping
against hope
to get out.

We watch,
outside the bars,
safe
in his imprisonment,
touched almost
by his sorrow,
reaffirmed
and comforted
by our victory.

Late one night
he finds a way
after years of searching
to get out.

He is hungry.
He hates.
He is coming
for you.

## WAR AND PEACE

Once you know war
you will never
know peace.

## WINTER PINES

The way pines sway
in winter's
cold sharp wind,
green gold against
a pale blue sky,

life against
non-life,
life fighting back,
bending but not
breaking,
knowing some day
it *will* break,
grow old and die,
and the winter wind
will take it down.

Sages in the pines
looking east
at sunrise splintered
through the branches,
sages gray with age,
with knowing
we shall all
be beaten down
like pines,
and when we vanish,
will it matter
that we lived?

## ROCK OF AGES

Take on your back
the rock of ages,
speak for everyone,
everywhere,
the past,
the present,
the future.

Speak for those
beyond time,
will never be,
or never were.

Speak for every living thing,
and every dead thing,
as if your voice only
will ever be heard,
so all truth survives
only in you.

There is a vision
of all time
and beyond all time,
of all spaces and dimensions
and beyond them.
Speak it.

## WE GIVE YOU THIS

We're so different, Abenaki.
Your world
was endless wilderness,
ours is endless
traffic, skyscrapers, strip malls,
TV and stop'n goes,
local parks
with seven trees
and a playground
full of dogshit.

We are so different,
Abenaki.
You had forests, lakes,
mountains, waterfalls
and sea –
this whole
religious extasy
of life.

We leave you the pines,
the flashing streams,
the wolves, caribou,
golden prairies,
silvery peaks,
wilds and woodlands
far beyond
endless horizons.

We keep
our filthy air,
constant crimes
and filthy food,
filthy noise
and filthy water,
your nomad paths
buried
under many billion tons
of asphalt and concrete.

We give you this:
You were wild, free,
and happy.

We are your
antithesis.

## CHILDREN OF THE ANTELOPE

When children
ran free
across golden prairies
seeking antelope
in tawny distance
or under the radiant shade
of cottonwoods,

when tall grass danced
in bright sun,
scented wind
riffled silver streams
and snapped at deerskins
in starlit night,

these memories
we can't forget,
these dreams we never
wished for,
even as the moon rises,
are gone,

gone the children
of the antelope
the dancing grass
the goddess moon
the fragrant wind
gleaming rivers
and brilliant night.

## LAUGHING GIRLS

How soon
laughing girls
are bent
old women

## LET US ALL

Kindness spreads –
do one good thing,
and another
is given you.

Unkindness spreads also –
cause pain,
and more pain
is given you.

Kindness
heals pain,
and pain
kills kindness.

So let us all
be kind.

## ALL LIFE

All life
is poetry;
the rest
is crap.

## DON'T SPEAK THE TRUTH

Don't speak the truth
and you will be lauded,
you will be loved
by a mob
who think
what they are told,
or they will put you
on the cross
that they detest
because they do not
understand,
because they do not
feel
except their own
worthy sorrow.

Don't speak the truth
or you will be silenced
because the mob fears
what they don't understand,

hates love,
hates attachment,
hates everything
they do not have,
and they do not have
anything.
Thus their hatred
is vast.

Go ahead,
speak the truth,
you will be blessed
and crucified.

## HOW CAN I NOT

In the verdant
spring
of living forever
in green fragrant
leaves, white peaks
and lovely
lissome sacred
women's bodies
opening to mine –
how could I not
be joyous,
how can I not,
now older,
love them still?

## FORESTS AND FIELDS

Eyes bathed in the beauty
of forests and fields,
of tender blue sky
beyond the fir peaks,

beavers, mink, moose, eagle
and so many more
living their lives
but fearing us too,

so many we kill,
and many more doom
over time,
the way galaxies die.

Each life, so
many lives,
raised with love,
vermin and human.

We must understand
the greatest power
is to care for life,
to nurture and give.

For every forest and field
bathed in sunset and mist,
fir crests and blue sky,
is given to us.

## WIDE RECEIVER

How I have loved football,
the fleeting downfield sprint,
the darting cut, raging breath,
fierce muscles,
soaring speed,
wild and free,
the arcing flight
of the ball
into my hands,
the safety's shuddering thud,
the crippling pain,
the staggering stumbling
escape
and saving moment
to the goal.

## HOW FAST

I'm so sorry
to have lived this.
It's branded
on my forehead
but only I
can see it:

    how fast
    a bullet
    kills you.

## DEEP WATER

Lying still
in deep water
I watch the wind
in the birch leaves
and understand
the universe.

## US GUYS

How we loved
football, fast cars,
wild women, wild drugs,
wild music, booze and fun,
loved hunting
steep rugged peaks
and starlit prairies,
our rough
hard friends,
and all
that gave us
life.

## THE CHOICE

The more you love
the more you have
to lose.

## LOOKING DOWN

Looking down
from piney hills
across great fields
of grain,
we see we once were
both wild and tamed –
once ate
what we hunted,
now hunted
by what we eat.

Once the forest
and wild prairies
were all we had,
and mountains too,
cold and remote,
where souls go
after death
to look down
on the world.

## NUCLEAR

We came down
from the trees
across the savanna
to new lands
and lives,
always with a stone
or club
or rifle
in our hands
to kill
each other,
and now
with a steel fire
to destroy the world
or travel
to new worlds
unknown?

Final war
or the universe,
which
shall it be?

## LUCKY OLD MAN

Happy old man,
happy with his children,
and grandchildren,
his beloved wife
of many years,
lucky old man.

## THE DANUBE

Truncated purple pillars of outcast stone,
the telephone a reason to live alone,
a door open to thieves and friends
and old maladies return to make amends,
politicians and the ungodly cheapest whores
sucking urine from the bread of bathroom floors –
all savage and serene, part time
between the vision and the vision's rhyme –
the reward for terror so easily espoused
darkens once more the rogue's black house.

## COLD HEART

There is somewhere
a cold heart
that counts our joys
and makes us pay.

## NOTRE DAME

In the end
all is lost,
even dreams
and ardent moments,
even our treasures
and our faith.

Notre Dame
our mother,
who brings life
into the world,
who *is* life,
lost
forever
from hatred
and stupidity.

Eight hundred years
of stone and oak
of loves and fears
and hopes and sorrows
embedded,
the memory
and proof,
of our past,
gone in hours
of foolish fancy.

Go ahead, mock.
Mock the faith
that birthed the modern world,
fertilized the future
with the promise of life.

Notre Dame,
we have lost our mother.
Woman,
giver of life,
its inspiration,
soul becoming body
down through millennia.

In the end
there will be no one.
Then nothing.

## TO SEE YOUR FACE

To see your face
across a room
delights my heart.

To hear your voice
makes my blood
sing.

To look
into your eyes
gives me wisdom.

To hold your hand
heats my soul
with love.

**FREE SPEECH**

There was once
free speech;
we said
what we thought.

We still have
free speech;
we can say anything
we're told to think.

## THE RIGHT TO KILL

We have the right
to kill a bird
once we can fly
like they do,
but not before.

We have the right
to kill a wolf
when we can live
as deep as he,
but not till then.

We have the right
to kill a man
after we've spent
a thousand days
in his skin.

We can kill
anyone we wish
if we can bring them
back to life.

We even have
a chance to love,
once we learn
to love ourselves.

## GIGONDAS

Poppies bloom
beneath an olive tree,
blood red below
silvery green leaves
along a gray stone wall,

flowers born
this spring,
the tree old
a thousand years,
the stone a hundred million,
though cut a mere
two thousand years ago
by human hand
to build a Roman fort,
reused a thousand years later
to build a castle,
and five hundred years
ago a wall.

So time betrays
and informs us,
we who rarely live
a hundred.

## WE ARE NOT HERE

We are not here
to be loved.
We are here
to love.

## LITTLE THINGS

We do little things
for each other,
heat coffee water,
move a pillow
from a chair,
buy something
the other wanted
but forgot.

Out of such
little things
comes great love.

## A ROOM OF DYING STRANGERS

Your look
across a room
of dying strangers –
they do not know,
or have forgotten.

Your touch
as if no one else
were here –
we're dying too,
but know.

## THE SACRED IS NOT SACRED

The sacred is not sacred
anymore,
the veils have fallen
between good and false,
all is profaned
and therefore equal,
and equally minimal,
neither profound
nor evil.
Do we celebrate
or weep?

**EVERY GOOD THING**

Every good thing
we do
is rooted
in death.

## GREAT MOMENTS

Nothing can be
what it was,
now and forever.

An elk amid
a golden field
at sunset.

A tropic bird
fork-tailed across
a blue noon sky.

Life in every humble
magic moment
of slime and stars.

Let us go on.
Great moments
await us.

## PEACE

Peace is
what is won
by combat.

## ARMED GUARDS

The rich
don't live like us.

They tell us
let everyone in,
the world's poor
gnashing at the gates,

while they live
behind tall walls
and armed guards;
they do not
deign
to travel
on our planes
that the fanatics
they embolden
try to destroy.

The rich
are better than we,
deserve more,
they say,
and take it.

## THE GREAT DIVIDE

Hand in hand
we face
the great divide

of woman
and man,
of life
and death,
joy
and sorrow.

One woman
one man
united
by flesh
and love
and memory
and children
across the years
till death
divides us
forever
or makes us
one.

## WAR IS

War is war.
Peace is
an illusion.

## THE SUN GOD

We
who have stripped ourselves
of the Gods
should remember
they are still with us,
they do not care
if we believe,
if we notice them,
if we thank them
or not.

The Sun God
rises every morning,
keeps our little earth
safe from ice
and barren stone.

The Moon Goddess
lights our path at night
and spares us
from the darkness.

There are many Gods;
the infinite universes
are full of them,

but we,
assured in our petty
mechanical knowledge,
do not recognize,
are not aware,
are not grateful,
for this brief
gift of life
that we can never
understand,
and will some day
pay the price.

## LIES

If we believe lies
we repeat them,
then others believe
and repeat them,
thus the vision
is lost,
and life
becomes a devious footnote
to some dusty text
long disrespected
and unloved.

## WHEN HAVE WE NOT

When have we not
had lots of opinions
nurtured by our favorite
firing squad?

## SOLACE

Without death
we could not know
we're alive.
Life would be
a constant state;
we would sense
nothing else.

Without death,
how could I love you
so deeply,
knowing I will
lose you?

Without light
there is no darkness,
without darkness
no light.

Without pain
no joy,
without joy
no pain.

This is no solace.
I would rather live forever,
loving you.

## JESUS NEVER WANTED

Jesus never wanted
servitude.
He never wanted love.
He felt sad
for us.

He was just
a desert straggler
trapped
in other people's
problems.

But he said
Do unto others,
and he said,
Do not harm,
and he said,
Love each other.

That's really all
Jesus ever said.
Or wanted.

## FUN

There is no
such thing
as too much.

## WHITE AND SILVER CLOUDS

White and silver clouds
over the mountains,
bare boughs and ice,
wind like a knife,
the gray light
of winter.

Be aware,
give thanks,
that in so many universes
of light and time
there should be this star
and a rock in space around it
circling just the right way
every year and day
to bring forth life.

Sun appears,
glitters off the ice,
a dead leaf flits past
on the wind
just like a bird.

The mountains are dark,
foreboding. Some day
we will go there.

And not come back.

# RENUNCIATION

The old sit quietly,
waiting for death,
spindly hands
and mottled skin
ready for the grave,
watery eyes fixed
on a screen, a window,
a distant past.

It hurts to remember,
so many try not to,
the present now
a soft cloud
of few sensations,
the past a lie,
a dream.

Chewing soft gums,
teetering
on aged bones,
it's hard to imagine
ardent kisses,
the throb of love,
children giggling,
a beloved young face,
voices, joys, and song,
green fragrant fields,
scarlet suns,
fir-clad peaks,
the soft delicious foam
of summer waves.

They may remember
and wish not to,
or have forgot
except inside
where perhaps
a seed of memory
persists.

We must not
be like this.
We must
fight death
with every tool and weapon,
aware
every day and night
how magical
life is.

And how evil
to lose it.

## EASY

It's so easy
to be nice
when you're rich.

Easy to pay debts,
love your kids,
your spouse.

Easy to clean house
(others do it),
feed your family.

Easy to go out
into the world
happy and free.

Why, then, are the rich
often not nice
or loving,
not happy, not free?

## CARAVANS

I would walk
a thousand miles
across the desert
for one instant
of her smile,

But she gives me caravans
of smiles,
vast moments
of joy
across great sands
of solitude.

Oh to love
and be loved –
what else?

## TROUBLE WITH NIRVANA

The trouble with nirvana
is we don't realize
we're there.

## WASP

A wasp
dying of winter
on my doorstep,
wishing to give him
a few more hours
of life,
not wanting
him to suffer,
I brought him
into the warmth.

He died anyway,
curling up
to sting himself
at the end.

## SEEING YOU

Seeing you
brings me joy,
no matter if I've been
seeing you
all day,
across the table,
in the car,
at the store,
in the bathroom
and kitchen
and everywhere else
we inhabit.

Seeing you
makes my heart leap
with gratitude,
no matter I saw you,
just moments ago,
if we'd been walking
hand in hand
across a parking lot
against the winter wind,
or trying to find the car keys,
or cooking, sleeping,
shoveling snow
or brushing teeth.

Sometimes at night
I see your sleeping face,
holy, wise and giving,
mother of tribes,

of such abundant love and kindness
there is plenty for everyone.
I have constantly, since we met,
loved you deeply and intensely,
but never more than now.

Seeing you
makes my heart beat
with steadiness
and eternity,
to know
that even time
may be defeated.

## SUN-WARM COFFEE

Sun-warm coffee
a stone terrace
over the sea

a diamond band
a distant boat
salt wind and lavender

a finch lands
grabs a crumb
and darts away

sky so blue
you can almost
see the stars

the boat's wake
a feather
on the horizon.

## TRUE LOVE

I tell her
she is perfect.
This annoys her,
but it's true.

## GRAY CLOUDS

Gray clouds above the dawn –
winter nears,
with spring just gone
and summer
not yet done.

Old age is like a child,
nervous and complaining,
needy and unknowing –
or knowing too much,
we'll never know.

And all that is accomplished
is dust.
And the only consolations
are blindness and forgetting.

I listen to the birds
and do not hear them –
caught as I am
in superficialities,
an early tractor,
a distant thrum,
the lights of human night
expiring,

distracted by the
meaningless parody
of human action.

There are times beyond
reconciliation
when each
must take the narrow path
of selfhood.

It is only then
that some dream
of constancy
is formed.

## SERMONS FOR THE POOR

Sermons for the poor
are good for the soul
of everyone else.

## THE SEXIEST GIRL IN FRANCE

When we were kids
we were doing it
all over the place,
back seats, pine-needled hills,
the ocean,
a lake, a river,
an airplane
going somewhere,

God, we had
a good time.
Now older
we look at each other
and grin,
not so long ago,
those days,
in the infinite turmoil
of the universe
it wasn't even
yesterday,
except we know
it was.

## FUCK DEATH

Fuck death,
the sorrow
of losing friends
and loved ones –
why wipe them out –
these brilliant loving
strong souls –
wasted
one by one?

No reason
no reason but
the spotted sails
at sunset,
entropy,
eternal change,
what God is that?

We rot and
turn to dust.
What God is that?

Death sucks.
Let us remember,
death sucks.
It is not necessary.

It is not good.
Better that we,
in our myriad
experiences,
love life,
live life
forever.

## WHEN YOU DO WRONG

When you
do wrong,
do right

## CLAIRE WAS NOT

Claire was not
her name,
but she was clear
as a bright blue mountain stream,
and cold as the ice
that made her.

## FUNNY

Funny,
to love someone
yet not know
where she is
right now.
Somewhere in the world,
airplanes, taxis, cafés,
three-star restaurants,
and hotels just for the night,
or part of it.

## TO HAVE A CAT

To have a cat
is to love death,
how she plays
with a dying robin,
her joy
when there's no hope.

To have a cat
is to live a moment
in our hopes
and fears,
our spendthrift love,
while the gaping jaws of death
smile down.

## SMILES

Her face smiles
but her heart
does not.

## THE GHOSTS OF DEER

The ghosts of deer
leave scent –
the dogs go mad
with hunting it.

We subdivide each other,
hanging the fixings over
the balcony ("il fait si
beau ici, par
la mer").

While our friends escape
in a stolen Rolls,
and crabs surprised
to waken on warm rocks
flit knowingly back
to the
sea.

## JOYOUS DAYS

These were the joyous days
ripped from the heart
of summer,
songs of youth
so soon extinguished,
the haughtiness of spring,
the slow assault
of fall,
then winter.

## LOVE

I would have walked
through fire
to the moon
for you.

I still will.

## SO COOL

We think we're cool
then death
gets us.

Till then it's what
we do
that counts.

## FRIENDS

A friend isn't someone
who asks for help,
who needs you.

A friend is someone
who needs nothing
from you,
or you from them.

A friend is someone
you give to,
because all love
is good.

## GIN

Few things
in the universe
are more valuable
than gin.

## ETERNITY LAUGHS

Long hair
let it down,
you
sacred soul
of magnificent beauty
for whom
my life throbs,
eternity laughs
in your eyes,
galaxies gleam
in your hair,
your touch
crosses universes
to reach me.

## SPIRIT AND FLESH

We all bemoan
the cross –
spirit and flesh,
we say,
as if they are not
the same,
as if
in our hungering
pursuit
for love hereafter
we do not love
each second
now
of raw sex
red wine
blood
bread
the beauty
of leaves
nodding in the wind,
and far mountains
of alabaster
and fir.

We all bemoan
death,
as we fear
the tiger
in the night,

the sharp knife
in the gut,
the beauty of eyes
that disdain us,
the hand
that chills,
the ice
that kills the trees
and cloaks the mountains
in the rime
of death.

Yes, we fear
the cross
and love death,
for are they not
the same?

## THE HUNT

Wind and sun in the pines
against a blue sky,
life and death
hunting each other
across the endless
dark.

## BELIEF

In India
children die
of hunger
on the sidewalk
while fat cows
walk the streets.

So does religion
steal our lives,
gives us instead
the fat cow
of belief.

## IN THE GREEN SPRINGTIME

In the green springtime
of our lives
how every breath
was perfumed,
every taste
sacred,
every moment
holy,
every love
intense,
and every second
gone forever.

## EVERY LOVE

Every love
kills another,
that's why
we call it
love.

## INNOCENT

The innocent
shall not be saved,
their hands
are drenched in blood,
their minds reek
of purity,
and sorrows
lie upon them
like the broken blanket
of faith.

**GOD**

That great enriching spirit
that animates
and destroys us.

## KILL THE OFFICE

Do not sit
in the vile stink
of others' breath
and farts
and sweat
and coffee,
plastic,
and the wretched
stench
of cities.

Do not inhale
the credence of crowds,
the sorrow of streetlights
in the rain,
and restaurants
and money
and sour subways
going nowhere.

We have one life
it is not meant
to be spilled
like martyr's blood
on the uncaring soil
of a forgotten desert

We have one life.

There are mountains
rivers
trees
seas
cold wind
dark-eyed loves
and hot nights
almost
without end.

Do not sit there,
love every moment
of joy and pain,
taste
the bitter poison
of freedom.

## WHERE IN THE UNIVERSE

The prettiest sight
in the universe
is your face,

the prettiest sound
your voice,

the most joyous is life
together,

and where
in the universe
do they go?

## CELEBRATION

Each day
the sun rises
a different way

Each flower
across the myriad
universe
of fields and forests
unique.

Each glance
across each face,
each delicate motion
of love

Each drop of rain
and breath
and quickening
pulse

Each instant grasped
from eternities
of love and fear.

## THE PASTS FORGETS

The past forgets itself,
turns to lies,
and like all liars
is believed,
until the curtain
rises,
but by then
it's far
too late.

## CANCEL

To cancel despair
we must first
cancel love.

## SHE FELL

She fell
for another,
and fell again,
the way
we all do,
not learning
till too late,
or not
at all.

Not learning
that there is really nothing
to learn,
when this universe
of our awareness
is circumscribed
by infinite
mystery,
and the big bang
of our creation
may also
be unreal.

So love
the forests
and fields,

the wild ones,
in their indescribable
beauty
and pure awareness,
the child
grown old
as we all do,
without understanding.

## WE ARE ALL BORN

It's easy
to get angry
at the imbecile
stupidity of us,
but remember:
we all are born
with a death sentence
on our heads.

## FOR THE MOMENT

Each night
the lake ice widens,
by dawn leaving
only a crack
of open water.

Then the sun
drives it back,
till night again
draws it closer.

Winter and summer,
on and on,
for the moment.

## GREEN BEAUTY

Wind in sunbright
morning leaves,
the promise of dawn,
days to come
of beauty and reverence,
the mystery
so clearly revealed
yet ineffable –
what choice do we have
but love it fully,
the evanescent
green beauty
of life?

## ROCK WALLS

The leaves, too,
are gone,
and winter winds
scurry round the roots;
we move closer
to the fire
in its bed of stones,
huddle closer
to the rock walls
that shelter us,
and wait.

## TWILIGHT OF THE GODS

Flies sparkling in setting sun
against a wall of trees,
dusk on gray bark,
glistening leaves,
the lurching of this earth
around a blazing sphere,
pounding blood, seeing,
hearing, breathing in –
all going to stop.

Every vision gone,
every love and heartache.
Be stoic,
but how?
How forgive
the loss of *this*?

To resign ourselves to death
devalues life,
as if it really doesn't matter,
that we're dying,
losing everything,
as if life isn't such a big thing, really.

I've seen a dying raccoon
fight off six dogs,
with feral hatred.
Two kids side by side
talking as they walk
down a rural road,
tan fields

and green forest
around them.

It would be good
to blame it on something,
a God perhaps –
so funny.

Even if we do persist
in some silly form,
where are fucking, eating,
sleeping in the sun and
every other bodily joy?

Not to mention roses,
and green and white mountains,
cliffs and far fine vistas of the seas,
salt air and bitter winters,
meat, fruit, blood and wine,
ardent moments like transitions
to another sphere?

The light-sparkling flies are gone,
the sun fallen
beyond the trees,
a cool stillness
in the breeze,
twilight,
the twilight of the gods
in every living thing.

## WARRIOR

I will die
as I have lived,
a warrior.

There is no other
life.

## STRONG

If you are strong
there is a reason.
Be happy.

If you are weak
there is a reason.
Learn it.

We can all
be strong
in our own way.

## ECOLOGY ACTION CANTATA

A leaf fell from a tree,
caught in a spider's web,
the spider had to go
and build another.

The Dutch sold Manhattan
to the Dutch, for 24 dollars
in beads, while its people
stood by, watching.

And who's to say
if concrete block, with its
regular indentation, is not all
we need.

The sky is bolder
now the trees are gone
I shall feed the field mice just
jello.

Such choice of roads
we have! In faith, were we wishing
to go somewhere it would not be hard
to get there! and

There is still the sea
in pockets, deep canyons on the floor

where we can lean over
and listen to the roar.

Indeed I feel a bit like Matthew Arnold:
such vice, so exotic, such
adventure
I can imagine,

For this celestial ball
has brought us change, has brought
us life, all new, all bright,
all revealing.

## THE OLD LANDMARK

There are no symbols
left, words prurient,
even eyes
are suspect.

Like centipede armies the
hiways under
cut hills, leaving
for a while stands of cañon oak
green over summer's brown grasses,
but of their own
inertia the hills
subside, the centipedes
rise slowly on more level
ground.

Any of us would kill
a native soon
as look at him,
rather than corral cattle
for part of an
afternoon.
We all drive
respectable pickups
painted flat
colors, talkin of the old
days
"D'in y'ever
get outta the saddle?"

We have good faces,
tanned,
open dark eyes a
smile a
hand on the shoulder

spurning as we
do the
ugly amongst us
(he leans from one back
to another engaging
momentary conversation)

with fascination we entertain
tales of other
lives
as steady as
our own
spiking what we trade with slight
exaggeration
chuckled
over
alone
as change
rattles on the counter

"When I die
I want a clean
hole – no lumps
in it."
"We're gonna bury you
standin up."

In a glass we cover
wars – second, first, between

"Them Spaniards still buried
under the bridge,"
friends come in to share
this shade
from Fourth
Street

there are no exaggerations
beyond our human pace,
all spirals, as the hawk's
end by finding
something,
the light
is cool here
streets far beyond and
out of notice,
our eyes have narrowed
to this darkness
where we wait,
darkness
where we sit
and wait,
predators
locked
from love,
locked in our last hunger
preceding
death

## BIRDS IN WINTER

Maybe it's not so bad
to nearly freeze to death
each night,
if that's the only life
you know.

And eventually,
one night
you do.

## ETERNITY

Your hand
your face
your eyes
your voice
are fine for me
for eternity.

## CRADLE TO GRAVE

Cradle to grave
we are drowning,
from the first moment
we choke for life,
death pushes us under,
and we fight back up,
only to be pushed down
again.

We tire,
each battle to the surface
harder,
each gasp
harsher,
and though we see
there is no shore
to swim to,
we still fight the waves,
the cold darkness,
the unknown,

sinking each time
deeper
till finally
like every drowner
we go down
and do not rise
again.

## THE LONG IS WIDER

The long is wider
than the wide,
as death is longer
than life.

See to the far edge
of every universe,
inside oneself
down to the core,
imagine
what it is
to be alive.

Or a star
or back to the start,
and on
to the end
of time
which is to a single moment
as the universe
is to a star.

## JUST BETWEEN

Just between
you and me
all belief
is pointless.
To believe in God
or nothing
depends on faith,
for we simply
do not know.

But I would not
be here
had not
some great power
time and time again
amid great dangers
delivered me
from death.

## NOTHING IS WHAT

Nothing
is what
it seems.

In the capital
politicians talk peace
but seek war.

Useless things
are sold
as good.

Life seems
to go forever
then stops.

Evil,
it is promised,
brings joy.

But your eyes
and you
are true.

And we die
but love
may live.

For at the end
nothing is
what it seems.

## END OF THE DAY

At the end of the day
when dusk cycles into dark
we light the candles
in our hearts
and pray for peace.

At the end of the day
the ravens gather, homeward,
wind rustles dead leaves
across deep snow,
deer huddle under hemlocks
and wait to die.

## DRUNK ON LIFE

We think we're sober
but we're not,
we never are
nor ever will –

drunk on life
until we die –
what good
is sober then?

## ENEMY

Government
is the protector
and enemy
of the people.

## THE CAVERN

Death gets us all,
the little girl
crossing the street,
the bald boy
dying of cancer,
the mother
and fallen soldier,
into the cavernous
maw
there is no end
but this.

## DUALITY

If there is a God
that God
must love
and hate us.

## EXTINCTION

How awful to lose
this sentient world,
this *everything*.

The lake glimmers through the trees,
infinite diamonds between the leaves,
a rustle of wind,
each breath,
the sun through clouds,
this table, deck, and earth –
all that surrounds us,
all that *is* us –
to vanish
as if it had
never been.

How awful to lose
this *everything*.
How can we describe it,
the fullness of our lives?
How much we can share,
that should not be thrown away?

When we cease to exist
does the world also
cease? As if we and all this
had never been?

By accident we step on an ant.
What *was* that life, so suddenly lost?
Are we the same?

## TRADEOFFS

To have joy
we must have sorrow,
for love
loss,
to have beauty
we must lose it,
and for pleasure
there is pain;
we live
but have to die.

## FATHER TO SON

We're here
such a short time,
and what we know
we keep inside,
generation to generation
never saying
the truth that death
rules us all,
every moment
waiting,
comes when it wants,
and all our glory,
love, patience,
duty and delight
are but a moment's whisper
in the night.

## IT'S EASY

It's easy
to be true
to falsehood,
say the right thing
for the wrong reasons,
to smile
with hatred,
to love
as does the viper
when she sinks death
into our hearts.

## MOMENTS

The moments flee,
the days and years,
was it true, ever,
that I loved you,
that we walked
the grass-strewn
prairies and tall mountains,
swam a thousand lakes,
and lived in every corner
of the world?

Is it true
that life goes on
without us
and everyone,
is there no sacred
any more?

Words do not
remain,
only nothing
remains,
which of itself
does not exist.

## PRESCRIBED

The pathways of the heart
have no rendition;
survival depends
on your condition,
a stone road
in Normandy,
a twisted path
in Maui or Baikal…
We are all one there
we follow the path
prescribed and unwavering
of total truth and lies.

## JOY IS

Joy is simple –
the smile
of a loved one,
an open field
in deep forest,
sunrise
on a snowy peak,
sunset
across the sea,
the laughter
of children,
birdsong,
and all the other
magical moments
in our lives.

## THE KNIFE OF LOVE

I love what kills me,
soaring slick cliffs
that terrify
and entrance me,
whose only way
is falling down,
wine and whisky
and all the drugs
that gently
still my heart,
the knife of love
that slips between my ribs,
the ancient sea
to vanish in
forever.

Life a combat
that kills at first a few,
then older, we watch
our friends
and loved ones die
all around us,
an ambush that
picks us off
one by one
till all we know
is death,
and the ardent memory
of what we lose.

## PLACES

A coral beach,
palms and a stream
sparkling
through the sand,
so sweet to drink

ridges of sharp firs
like marching soldiers,
white peaks and
granite sheen
across blue lakes

green-gold prairies,
seas of flowers,
ruby hills,
bird clouds and antelope
to the horizons

Paris at dawn
the Tower aflame
with new sun,
and every other place
to love
on earth.

## MAGIC

You are the magic
of my life;
the music plays,
the moon
is nearly full,
and death waits
at our door
like an indolent stranger.

## OWN

Whatever
you own
owns you.

## MAIMED BY TIME

He stands there,
beaten as a man
can be,
and yet
he stands there

about to die
in the vast horror
of it.

They have killed
his wife
and children.

A carpenter,
he built a life
as sacred
as the homes he made,
now all
destroyed.

He is patient,
waiting to die.
The hatred
he bears them
will outlast
time.

## MORE

The more we love
the more
is given us
to love.

## PALEOLITHIC TV

A campfire is
paleolithic TV,
ever changing,
always the same –
heat, love,
comfort and safety,
a universe
of visions
and truth.

## SURVIVAL

The days pass
like dead leaves
washing down a culvert
in the first days
of winter.

One is like
another, except for those
who die.

We are happy
and sad,
resolute
and fearing
to our last day.

So are the other
animals, perhaps even
the stones,
the earth itself,
the universe.

No point in wondering
why
except it feeds
a very slim chance
of survival.

## NOTHING LESS

We should all
seek the infinite,
and take
nothing less.

**PITY THOSE**

Pity those
who die young,
never see
youth's sunrise
fade to dusk,
how bright bodies
turn to pain,
how even love
grows mortal.

## RAIN

Down urgent streams
and mountain forests
life flows,
through stark canyons
and vast prairies,
under bird clouds
and granite cliffs,
over ancient lakes
and vanished peaks
to the sea,
which gives it back
as rain.

## RECKONING

You,
blessed soul,
as you touch
a child's head
or search for a piece
of missing puzzle,

you, hand akimbo
as you lean
over the box
of infinite
puzzle pieces,
your long tangled
auburn hair
hanging free.

We are
God knows what,
or are we?

Softness in the wind,
the time of reckoning
is near.

## SACRED

The person you love
becomes sacred
by your love,
and because
they are sacred
there is nothing
you should do
to harm them.

We live a while
then turn to dust,
but nothing
can outlast time
like love.

## SADNESS

How can we not
be sad,
if we love
life?

## SEMBLANCE

You touch my wrist,
I hold your hand
and feel the skin,
muscles, tendons,
flesh and blood,
the nerves that take me
to your heart,
your mind and brain.

We are but a semblance
of who we are,
the mind, the smile,
the caring, love,
sorrow and hate –
they are not us –
flesh and bone, love
and love lost
forever.

## FIVE HUNDRED YEARS

An oak old
five hundred years
killed by a man
who'll live seventy,

burned in his stove
to keep him alive
a few more days
of his life.

## SOMETIMES

Sometimes
I'm so unhappy
as to break
the universe
in half.

## SPECIAL MOMENTS

Life will teach us
not to be sorry
for what we have
not done.

Life will teach us
not to be sorry –
it will beat us down
with so much sorrow
we no longer fear
or care –
except in special moments
when we remember death.

Life will beat us down
with so much joy
that losing it
will kill us.

Life will teach us
with so much beauty
that every instant
has promise
if we only
know.

## WISDOM

Time ends
very soon
so use it
wisely.

## SWEET JESUS OF THE MOUNTAINS

Sweet Jesus of the mountains
hungry for the hand
that holds me
at your side,
warm the fire of night
out of the far depth
of this universe,
this home,
God of love, of giving,
god of warm hands,
warm side,
warm repetition,
in and out the cave
of darkness
take you me
now and forever.

## IN ALL THIS UNIVERSE

In all this universe
what are we,
me and you?

Crags of bone, muscle
and grit, old miracles
and memories, cells,
blood, neurons –
shoulder bones and brain –
all physical.

But what are we?
And who?

## TIME

How the clock rambles,
counting hours, minutes,
moments in our lives
till we unplug it.

## LONG DARK NIGHT OF THE SOUL

What do we pray for,
when we learn
there is nothing?

To be cast out
into this universe
of fire and ice?

To rot beneath the earth,
perhaps dug up some day
by strangers?

To be forgotten,
when there is no one
left to forget?

To sorrow forever
for what we've done,
and not done?

To live again,
remembering
nothing?

Death does not exist,
because we cannot
comprehend it?

Death exists,
it is we
who soon will not.

## THE WAR OF LIFE

The war of life
drives us
together and apart
like refugees
hunted from our homes,
we flee
to new unknowns
starved
for knowledge
and peace.

## TRY

We must try
all our lives
to understand
what we can never
understand

## APPLE-WOOD BUFFET

An apple-wood buffet
alive three hundred years,
cut and chiseled
with bare hands
and great love –
how many souls
have touched you?
How many hearts
have loved you?
How many thousand hours
have been lived
by your side?

Where are they
now?

## VIPER

The viper
says
she loves you.

The viper
never lies.

## WE PRAISE

We praise the good
in those who've died
because the good
is what we love
in ourselves.

## FLASH IN THE NIGHT

How can I love
you so
if we are just
a flash in the night?

How can we all
live so hard
if we are but
a flash in the night?

How can you and I
hand in hand
face, without relenting,
the everlasting end?

Oh Lord
please tell me,
or are you too
just a flash in the night?

## WISDOM AND HEART

There is always
a reason
to kill.
There are always
reasons
to die.
Wisdom and heart
tell us
refuse both.

## PITILESS

The good thing
about life
is that it's
pitiless.

## APART AND ONE

Years ago
we were wild hot
young lovers,
couldn't get
enough of each other,
we still can't,
but far older,
always still thinking
of each other,
cherishing each
moment,
facing death
together,
though each
will die alone.

We are the same
and different:
love does this.

We are apart
and one.

## BUT FOREVER

There is no future
but the past,
no never
but now,
no instant
but forever.

## A LONG TIME

Forever is not
a long time
when you don't
have a long time.

## LET THE PAST GO

Let the past go,
it doesn't live here any more,
what lives here now
is also past,
all that lasts
is future.

## RETROSPECT

When I walked young
and howled among the trees,
tall
was I then, and how
I slashed at them,
bleeding white,
silver on bark.

Now older, I stand alone,
and wish them back.

## SLOWING TIME

Seeking completeness
in objects
is delaying death –
not living longer,
but simply slowing time
through dullness.

## MY FAITH COMETH

Out of the long silent columns
of the hills
my faith cometh.

Out of tall pines swaying
in winter wind,
the coyote's howl,
your eyes seeing
into mine,
the laughter
of a child,
an old man's
dying cough,
the rising
of the sun
and its setting
each new night
cometh my faith.

## THE ONLY

The only changeless thing
in the universe
is change.

## BARE TREES

Bare trees
of winter,
new ice
on the lake,
dying coals
in the west

Cold closes in,
the ice
cracks and hardens,
the pines darken
among bare birch
and beech and oak
against the silver night

The stars grow strong
amid the branches,
the night turns black,
the universe widens
deepens
goes on without end

## GRASS IN THE WIND

Grass blows in the wind,
eternity beckons
and recedes.

## MIRACLES

We are all
miracles.
So let us love
each other.

## WIND IN THE LEAVES

Wind moves the leaves
they shatter with light
against tall black trunks.

Galaxies rise and fall,
women cry out,
children die.

Mountains wash down
into the seas
and rise again
beneath them.

Take a breath,
the world is new,
and ever the same.

# ABOUT THE AUTHOR

First published by Lawrence Ferlinghetti in City Lights Books, Mike Bond is an award-winning poet, best-selling novelist, ecologist, and war correspondent.

He has been called *"the master of the existential thriller"* (BBC), *"one of America's best thriller writers"* (Culture Buzz), *"a nature writer of the caliber of Matthiessen"* (WordDreams), and *"one of the 21st century's most exciting authors"* (Washington Times).

He has covered wars, revolutions, terrorism, military dictatorships and death squads in the Middle East, Latin America, Asia and Africa, and environmental issues including elephant poaching, habitat loss, wilderness survival, whales, wolves and many other endangered species.

His novels place the reader in intense experiences in the world's most perilous places, in dangerous liaisons, political and corporate conspiracies, wars and revolutions, making *"readers sweat with [their] relentless pace"* (Kirkus) *"in that fatalistic margin where life and death are one and the existential reality leaves one caring only to survive."* (Sunday Oregonian).

He has climbed mountains on every continent and trekked more than 50,000 miles in the Himalayas, Mongolia, Russia, Europe, New Zealand, North and South America, and Africa.

Author Website and Contact:
www.mikebondbooks.com

For film, translation or publication rights,
or for interviews contact:
Meryl Moss Media
meryl@merylmossmedia.com or 203-226-0199

## POETRY

### THE DRUM THAT BEATS WITHIN US

The tradition of the poet warrior endures throughout human history, finding expression in the Bible's King David, the Vikings of Iceland, Japan's Samurai, the Shambhala teachings of Tibet, the ancient Greeks and medieval knights. *"The Drum That Beats Within Us presents us with a world gone awry, a world in which the warrior poet has fought, and a world in which only love survives." – VINE REVIEWS* ... "A joy to read." *– BOOKTRIB* ... "Exquisite... written from the heart." *– LIBRARY THING*

### NOVELS

### AMERICA *(America series Book 1)*

Vietnam, civil rights, rock'n roll, free love and wild drugs are woven into a 1960s epic. From rural farm life, two girls and two boys take different paths – the Marines, the peace movement, a rock band, and scientific research on hallucinogens. Celebrated author Mike Bond's *America,* the first in his seven-volume historical novel series, captures the victories and heartbreaks of the last 70 years and our nation's most profound upheavals since the Civil War. "A coming-of-Age Masterpiece." *– ST. LOUIS POST-DISPATCH*

## FREEDOM *(America series Book 2)*

From the war-shattered jungles of Vietnam to America's burning cities, near-death in Tibet, peace marches, the battle of the Pentagon, wild drugs, rock concerts, free love, CIA coups in Indonesia and Greece, the Six Days' War, and Bobby Kennedy's last campaign, *Freedom* puts you in the Sixties as if it were now. "The characters are so vivid and alive, you think you're reading about old friends and recalling fond memories of youth." – *THE TIMES-NEWS ONLINE*

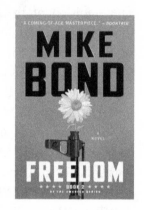

## REVOLUTION *(America series Book 3)*

The late 1960s shook America to its foundation, from peace marches to the battle of Hué, CIA coups, riots in Motown to onstage at Woodstock, Zen monasteries, the Six Days' War, Paris street battles, Martin Luther King is shot, and riots rage in 130 burning American cities. Students take over American universities, Bobby Kennedy is shot, and the threat of civil war darkens the nation. "A fascinating read from cover to cover... highly recommended." – *MIDWEST BOOK REVIEW*

## THE LAST SAVANNA

FIRST PRIZE FOR FICTION, *Los Angeles Book Festival*: "One of the best books yet on Africa, a stunning tale of love and loss amid a magnificent wilderness and its myriad animals, and a deadly manhunt through savage jungles, steep mountains and fierce deserts as an SAS commando tries to save the elephants, the woman he loves and the soul of Africa itself." Also, "One of the most realistic portrayals of Africa yet… Dynamic, heart-breaking and timely to current events… a must-read." – *YAHOO REVIEWS*

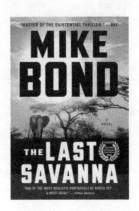

## ASSASSINS

From its terrifying start in Afghanistan to its stunning end in the Paris terrorist attacks, an insider's account of the last 30 years of war between Islam and the West. A US commando, an Afghani warlord, a French woman doctor, a Russian major, a CIA spy and a British woman journalist fight for their lives and loves in the lethal deserts of the Middle East. "An epic spy story of political intrigue, religious fanaticism, love, brotherhood, and the ultimate pursuit of Peace." – *HONOLULU STAR ADVERTISER*

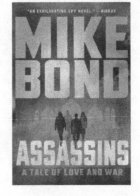

**SAVING PARADISE** *(Pono Hawkins Book 1)*

When Special Forces veteran Pono Hawkins finds a beautiful journalist drowned off Waikiki he is quickly caught in a web of murder and political corruption. Trying to track down her killers, he finds them hunting him, and blamed for her death. "An action-packed, must read novel ... taking readers behind the alluring façade of Hawaii's pristine beaches and tourist traps into a festering underworld of murder, intrigue and corruption." – *WASHINGTON TIMES* ... "A rousing crime thriller." – *BOOK CHASE*

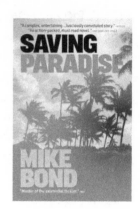

**KILLING MAINE** *(Pono Hawkins Book 2)*

**FIRST PRIZE FOR FICTION**, *New England Book Festival.* "A gripping tale of murders, manhunts and other crimes set amidst today's dirty politics and corporate graft, an unforgettable hero facing enormous dangers as he tries to save a friend, protect the women he loves, and defend a beautiful, endangered place." ..."Quite a ride for those who love good crime thrillers." – *BOOK CHASE* ... "Another terrifically entertaining read from a master of the storytelling craft." – *MIDWEST BOOK REVIEW*

**GOODBYE PARIS** (*Pono Hawkins Book 3*)

Special Forces veteran Pono Hawkins races from Tahiti to France when he learns a terrorist he'd thought was dead has a nuclear weapon to destroy Paris. Alive with covert action and insider details from the war against terrorism, *Goodbye Paris* is a hallmark Mike Bond thriller: tense, exciting, and will keep you up all night. "A rip-roaring page-turner." – *CULTURE BUZZ* ... "Another non-stop thriller of a novel by a master of the genre." – *MIDWEST BOOK REVIEW* ... "A stunning thriller." – *BOOKTRIB*

**SNOW**

Three hunters steal $10 million in cocaine from a crashed plane in the Montana wilderness, and are soon pursued by the Mexican cartel, the DEA, Las Vegas killers, and the FBI. From the frozen peaks of Montana to Wall Street, the Denver slums and million-dollar Vegas tables, *Snow* is "a captivating story." – *KIRKUS* ... "An action-packed adventure, but also a morality tale of what happens when two men who should know better get entangled in a crime from which they can't escape." – *DENVER POST*

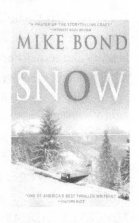

## HOUSE OF JAGUAR

Based on the author's experiences as the last foreign journalist alive in Guatemala after over 150 journalists had been killed by death squads. A terrifying thriller of CIA operations in Latin America, guerrilla wars, drug flights, military dictatorships, environmental catastrophes and death squad genocides. "A high-octane story rife with action, from U.S. streets to Guatemalan jungles." – *KIRKUS* ... "A riveting thriller of murder, politics, and lies." – *LONDON BROADCASTING*

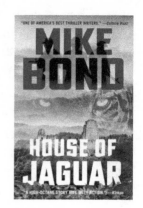

## HOLY WAR

Based on the author's experiences in the Battle of Beirut – an American spy, a French commando, a Palestinian woman guerrilla, a Hezbollah terrorist and a brilliant teacher are all caught in a crossfire of love and war on the deadly streets and fierce deserts of the Middle East. "Action-filled thriller." – *MANCHESTER EVENING NEWS (UK)* ... "A stunning novel of love and loss, good and evil." – *GREATER LONDON RADIO* ... "A profound tale of war." – *BRITISH ARMED FORCES BROADCASTING*

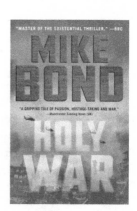

## TIBETAN CROSS

A terrifying international manhunt and stunning love story. An American climber in the Himalayas stumbles on a shipment of nuclear weapons headed into Tibet for use against China. Pursued by spy agencies and other killers across Asia, Africa, Europe and the US, he is captured then rescued by a beautiful woman with whom he forms a deadly liaison. They escape, are captured and escape again, death always at their heels. "Grips the reader from the opening chapter and never lets go." – *MIAMI HERALD*

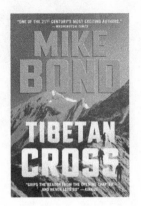

CPSIA information can be obtained
at www.ICGtesting.com
Printed in the USA
BVHW042300171222
654484BV00005B/307